Legends of the T.T.
Art, Facts, & Fun!

Created by Max. M. Power

With artwork by Peter Hearsey

This publication is part of a series of products and publications. For

more information, please visit: www.racingbooks.org

Published in 2019 By The 3 A's Group

ISBN: 9781097571994

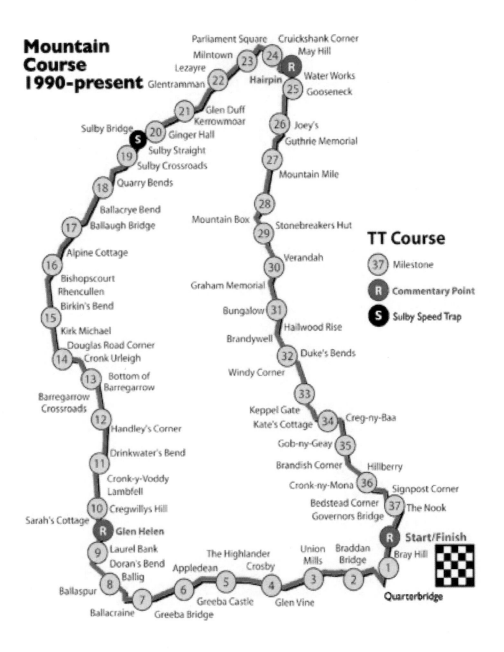

Mountain Course 1990-present

Parliament Square — Cruickshank Corner
Milntown — 23 — 24 — May Hill
Lezayre — 22 — R — Water Works
Glentramman — Hairpin — 25 — Gooseneck
21 — Glen Duff — 26 — Joey's
Kerrowmoar — Guthrie Memorial
Sulby Bridge — 20 — Ginger Hall — 27
19 — S — Sulby Straight — Mountain Mile
Sulby Crossroads — 28
18 — Quarry Bends — Mountain Box — 29 — Stonebreakers Hut
Ballacrye Bend — Verandah
17 — Ballaugh Bridge — 30
Alpine Cottage — Graham Memorial
16 — Bungalow — 31 — Hailwood Rise
Bishopscourt — Brandywell
Rhencullen — 32 — Duke's Bends
Birkin's Bend — Windy Corner
15 — 33
Kirk Michael — Keppel Gate — 34 — Creg-ny-Baa
Douglas Road Corner — Kate's Cottage
14 — Cronk Urleigh — Gob-ny-Geay — 35
13 — Bottom of Barregarrow — Brandish Corner — Hillberry
Barregarrow Crossroads — Cronk-ny-Mona — 36
12 — Bedstead Corner — 37 — Signpost Corner
Handley's Corner — Governors Bridge — The Nook
Drinkwater's Bend — R — Start/Finish
11 — Union Mills — Braddan Bridge — Bray Hill
Cronk-y-Voddy — The Highlander — 1
Lambfell — Crosby
10 — Cregwillys Hill — Appledean — 5 — 4 — 3 — 2
Sarah's Cottage — 6 — Glen Vine
R — Glen Helen — Quarterbridge
9 — Laurel Bank
Doran's Bend — 7
8 — Ballig
Ballaspur — Greeba Castle
Ballacraine — Greeba Bridge

TT Course

37 Milestone

R Commentary Point

S Sulby Speed Trap

The excellent Peter Hersey prints shown here can be purchased from Duke Marketing. https://www.dukevideo.com/Isle-of-Man-TT

Introduction

*I'm sitting on the start line, first away, the black strip of road
stretching out before me tapers to a distant point. All is silent. Deep
breath...the pungent smells of oil, petrol and rubber invade my
senses. Leather clad hands gripping the rubber handle bars. My
stomach is churning with a mix of excitement and fear.*
Why do we do this I would rather be anywhere but here?
*The starter drops his flag I run with the bike, pushing fast, drop onto
the saddle and the engine screams into life.*

For more than 100 years every rider who starts out over their
first lap of the thirty-seven-and-a-half-mile lap of the Isle of Man
mountain course has similar thoughts. For all riders a TT win is
the achievement of a lifetime's ambition.
The races are the ultimate test of riders and machines and have
contributed enormously to motorcycle development. Victories in an Isle
of Man Tourist Trophy race have made British manufactures like
Norton, Triumph and Matchless world famous.
To race at the Isle of Man a rider must accept the ever-present
dangers. Natural hazards like walls, kerbs, banks, lamp posts,
and steep unprotected drops off the mountain section make this
a unique place in today's safety obsessed world. No run-off areas
here!

This small book does not pretend to be a history of the TT. There are
excellent books full of comprehensive records and fascinating tales of
the dramas, successes and failures in this great event. We have listed
some recommended reading towards the end of this book. In here we
have a celebration of many of the riders the TT has turned into heroes,
plus interesting, fun based, puzzles for you to solve while you wait for
the next howl of a screaming racing engine to pass by.

Extract from "A Fatal Addiction". The Triumphs and the Tragedies

"Head down, chin grazing the petrol tank of his black Norton, he sets out on his last thirty-seven-mile lap. Flat out down Bray Hill, the heat from the screaming engine intense, the stinging flies and dirt peppering his face. The sign his mechanic Pete gives him as he flashes past the pits confirm he is leading by ten seconds.

Throttle twisted wide open as he rushes round the bends at Quarter and Bradden Bridges, Ballacraine, Kirk Michael, the Ramsey hairpin all pass. Up on the mountain now, through the Gooseneck, and the Bungalow and Windy Corner. Charging down to Creg-ny-Baa, braking hard, rear wheel sliding round the righthand bend. Now plunging down to Brandish Corner, on to Hilberry and around Governor's Bridge hairpin. Twist the throttle wide open, faster, and faster, the finish line in sight, flash under the waving Chequered flag...Thirty-seven and half miles of joy".

An exclusive print by renowned artist Peter Hearsey produced to commemorate the 90th anniversary of the TT. Rem Fowler is pictured at St. Johns on his Peugeot Norton at the start of the first ever TT Race in 1907. He won the Twin-Cylinder Class and rode on this course until 1910, then competed in the first races on the Mountain Course in 1911. Each 594mm x 420mm print is personally signed by the artist and is one of limited editions of 850.
https://www.dukevideo.com/prd8770/TT-Legends-Rem-Fowler-Print

The following words can be found in the diagram below reading forward, backward, up, down and diagonally. Find the words and circle them.

hailwood	chain
misfiring	entry
spectators	broken
accident	trophy
speed	ivy
tyres	redman

```
S X E L H V C B J Z O P J M X A
R I Z T S M M J R Z O F M N C K
O V A B P W Y T H G T P J C H D
T Y Z J V P T I M S Y B I F F O
A N O W N D C Z R N R D A S C O
T W R R V E X L O E E K Y A A W
C R E I N K K S G N S P Y H L L
E L D L O L C N T B L V D I N I
P Z M M K L I B P W Z P W R Y A
S J A B N R J B R H J D T U R H
E X N T I P T W X G W K R E H M
G D L F A W Z D U I F E K N X L
U A S E H O S J M L Z G I T X N
E I H E C M T L P N E K O R B F
M H P J C Y O G I L R C M Y W R
E S P E E D G E Q T R O P H Y F
```

Freddie Dixon on his 500cc Indian on the approach to Ballig Bridge chasing a fellow competitor on his way to second place in the 1921 Senior Race. He won the first ever Sidecar TT in 1923 with the famous Douglas 'banking' outfit to become the only rider to win solo, sidecar and car TT's.

This print has been signed by the artist and is one of a Limited Edition of 850.
594 mm x 420 mm
https://www.dukevideo.com/prd8778/TT-Legends-Freddie-Dixon-Print

Each of these Cryptograms is a message in substitution code. THE SILLY DOG might become UJD WQPPZ BVN if U is substituted for T, J for H, D for E, etc. One way to break the code is to look for repeated letters. E, T, A, O, N, R and I are the most often used letters. A single letter is usually A or I; OF, IS and IT are common 2-letter words; try THE or AND for a 3-letter group. The code is different for each Cryptogram.

1. Vnaczakch bnn owpb K vawpuzs kcbn
   buz lwcg, xwp xkcszs wcs bnaz ym
   qzwbuzap lwsqm

2. Mwzu wej qkxbzj bzku lerm da
   qkegmdgz, fnm wej wej e ledk esxnam
   xl szgweadgeo mkxnfoz.

3. Mxx uew amqktz bjswbz pwbw kv uew
   ibjs, mvs mxx uew amqktz gjfwz.

Here Peter Hearsey has captured Stanley Woods negotiating Quarterbridge on his 350cc Velocette in the 1938 Junior - the race that gave him his ninth TT victory. His first win was the 1923 Junior on a Cotton and the last of his 10 wins was the 1939 Junior. Each 594mm x 420mm print is signed by the artist and is one of a limited edition of 850.
https://www.dukevideo.com/prd8771/TT-Legends-Stanley-Woods-Print

Insert a different letter of the alphabet into each of the 26 empty boxes to form words reading across. The letter you insert may be at the beginning, the end or the middle of the word. Each letter of the alphabet will be used only once. Cross off each letter in the list as you use it. All the letters in each row are not necessarily used in forming the word.

Example: In the first row, we have inserted the letter Z to form the word BENZOL

A B C D E F G H I J K L M N O P Q R S T U V W X Y Z̸

U	W	H	B	E	N	**Z**	O	L	H	R	I	L
T	Q	S	D	X	Y		N	T	R	Y	V	W
V	C	P	R	E	D		A	N	W	D	T	O
P	B	I	D	R	O		E	N	N	E	T	T
F	M	H	A	I	R		I	N	J	Q	S	E
B	P	Z	R	O	A		O	G	H	M	X	W
E	L	B	P	O	S		T	I	O	N	A	E
X	W	M	A	T	C		L	E	S	S	Y	D
F	Y	I	R	R	E		O	R	D	T	G	K
R	T	H	O	S	E		E	C	T	C	L	N
V	H	I	R	T	H		N	D	E	R	N	U
W	E	A	T	H	E		S	N	W	V	C	T
K	U	J	H	U	S		V	A	R	N	A	B
V	K	Y	E	N	P		U	E	L	S	T	O
W	A	C	P	F	I		I	S	H	D	N	C
O	N	A	R	R	O		P	A	C	M	V	E
N	L	F	V	O	I		T	C	F	R	Y	D
L	A	P	P	I	N		A	L	I	H	W	K
Q	H	A	I	L	W		O	D	X	U	R	V
G	E	A	R	B	O		F	T	B	M	O	X
G	S	W	J	G	R		I	N	F	S	Z	W
N	J	S	U	Z	U		I	R	B	Y	K	U
X	T	R	O	P	H		Z	X	V	M	O	Q
K	A	M	O	U	N		A	I	N	Y	N	Q
A	E	N	E	O	H		I	C	T	O	R	Y
S	U	R	T	E	E		Y	W	H	U	W	K

10

Omoboni Tenni on his 250cc Moto-Guzzi cornering at Hillberry on his way to victory in the 1937 Lightweight when this was a second gear corner! He became the first foreign rider to win the Lightweight TT.
This print is just one of an exclusive set of twelve by renowned artist Peter Hearsey Each print has been signed by the artist and is one of a Limited Edition of 850. 594mm x 420mm.
https://www.dukevideo.com/prd8772/TT-Legends-Omobono-Tenni-Print

Solve each clue to produce a word that will fit in the corresponding boxes.

ACROSS WORDS
1 - This Is Carl
2 - World Champ. On Two & Four
7 - Field Plowing Team
8 - You Can Take Off Here
10 - Really Gets To
11 - Pajama Topper
12 - A Jazzy Kind Of Singing
13 - Back Of The Neck
15 - The Yellow Cab Is This
16 - Reason To Darn A Stocking
17 - Rewrite

18 - Motes
19 - Row; Level
20 - Abominable Snowman
24 - Avenue
25 - Bread Comes As This
26 - Worshipped Object
27 - Jimmie Of The Norton Team
28 - Come Down From Above

DOWN WORDS
1 - It's The End.
3 - They Line The Track

4 - The Greatest Italian Rider
5 - They Grip The Track
6 - You Get This For Victory
9 - A Famous British Bike
14 - One Mistake Can Cause This
21 - Great USA Bike
22 - Bill, Small But Very Quick
23 - Exciting
20 - Jefferies Won On These

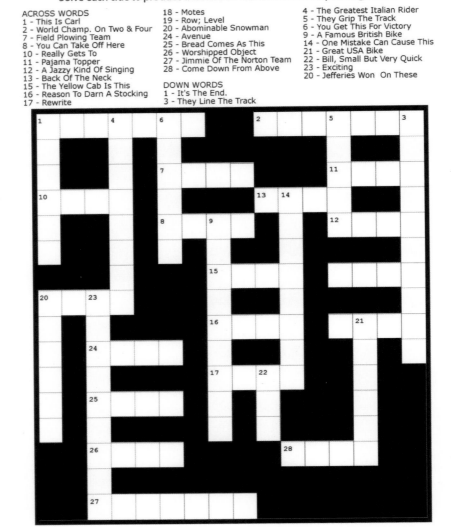

Walter Zeller had to wrap himself around his 500cc B.M.W. machine - as this Windy Corner shot shows! He only competed in three Senior T. T. Races in 1955, 1956 & 1957. He had 2 retirements but took a magnificent 4th place in the 1956 Senior. Each print has been signed by the artist and is one of a Limited Edition of 850. 594mm x 420mm.
https://www.dukevideo.com/prd8779/TT-Legends-Walter-Zeller-Print

The spaces between the words in the following message have been eliminated and divided into pieces. Rearrange the pieces to reconstruct the messages. The dashes indicate the number of letters in each word.

```
EDBY  SOTH  EROF  NGSE  MEMB  ANEX
ENOR  SDIS  TONW  QUEN  ROWN  TEAM
INNI  TURB  CEWA  THEI
```

__ __   __ __ __   __ __ __ __ __ __

__ __ __ __ __ __ __

__ __ __ __ __ __ __ __

__ __ __   __ __ __ __ __ __ __ __ __ __

__ __   __ __ __   __ - __ __ __ __ __ __

__ __   __ __ __ __ __

__ __ __   __ __ __ __ __ .

Bob McIntyre on his 500cc Gilera. During the T.T.'s 50th Anniversary, history is made - the first official 100mph lap in the 1957 Senior TT.

It was an eight lap race and Bob is pictured completing a Senior/Junior double on the fabulous Gilera at Quarterbridge.

Each print has been signed by the artist and is one of a Limited Edition of 850. 594mm x 420mm.

https://www.dukevideo.com/prd8774/Bob-McIntyre-TT-Legend-Print

The following words can be found in the diagram below reading forward, backward, up, down and diagonally. Find the words and circle them.

grant	snaefell
agusta	lapping
programme	prize
petrol	track
matchless	suzuki
honda	oil

```
L  Q  Y  D  L  L  E  F  E  A  N  S  J  D  G  A
O  A  Z  W  S  Y  N  J  V  L  A  Z  X  S  A  G
Q  C  P  D  K  Q  U  Z  E  T  G  H  W  K  G  R
A  U  K  P  G  U  Z  F  Q  S  U  Z  U  K  I  A
S  D  P  R  I  Z  E  E  B  Z  S  P  A  W  I  N
B  N  K  E  Y  N  B  Z  X  F  T  T  F  C  D  T
M  C  Y  X  J  T  G  W  P  K  A  P  T  O  Q  S
D  R  P  M  S  C  S  W  X  B  X  W  Z  D  Q  F
F  T  R  H  S  P  R  S  L  L  G  V  B  Z  J  R
R  N  I  G  Z  B  J  W  E  Z  K  U  V  K  X  L
P  D  F  H  K  Y  W  C  J  L  I  O  I  I  E  P
J  H  O  A  Z  B  J  F  A  L  H  O  X  K  Z  E
R  G  J  P  R  Y  S  X  G  D  V  C  C  F  E  T
K  O  J  T  T  R  A  C  K  V  X  U  T  U  Z  R
E  A  A  H  O  N  D  A  P  P  X  Z  P  A  P  O
F  Y  E  E  M  M  A  R  G  O  R  P  X  X  M  L
```

Here we see Geoff Duke O.B.E. flat out on his 350cc Norton at 120mph on the approach to Ballacraine during the 1951 Junior TT. Geoff went on to win this race and the 1951 Senior TT, as well as both 1951 World Championships. Geoff won a total of 6 TT's and 6 World Championships before retirement in 1959. He was Sportsman of the Year and awarded the Segrave Trophy in 1951, received the O.B.E. from Queen Elizabeth in 1953

and is a MotoGP Legend. Each 594mm x 420mm print is personally signed by the artist and is one of a limited edition of 850. Only 100 have been signed by Geoff Duke himself so this is a very rare opportunity to acquire a highly collectable piece of art.
https://www.dukevideo.com/prd8781X/TT-Legends-Geoff-Duke-Print

Geoff Duke thunders down Bray Hill on his 500cc Norton during the 1950 Senior TT. A Limited Edition of 500 A4 prints were produced and signed by Geoff on the occasion of his 80th birthday in 2003.
https://www.dukevideo.com/prd8781A4/Geoff-Duke-TT-Legend-A4-Signed-Print

Each of these Cryptograms is a message in substitution code. THE SILLY DOG might
become UJD WQPPZ BVN if U is substituted for T, J for H, D for E, etc. One way to break
the code is to look for repeated letters. E, T, A, O, N, R and I are the most often used
letters. A single letter is usually A or I; OF, IS and IT are common 2-letter words; try THE or
AND for a 3-letter group. The code is different for each Cryptogram.

1. Uff xjv kuylzh bgwvbh qvbv ls xjv
   cbgw, usw uff xjv kuylzh ogpvh.

2. Xsrur fur tra viflrw asrur xsr upcru
   pw qjx dfqgrc jyru jqr wpcr ju xsr
   jxsru.

3. G eseryugd fdgjos agn fdghsw rb kps
   agdd rffrnuks kps nkgyk dubs.

Here is John Surtees on his 500cc Norton at Windy Corner during practice for his first TT in 1954. In 1956 he won his first race - the Senior. Altogether he notched up six TT wins between 1956 and 1960 and became the first rider to score a hat-trick of Senior wins. Each 594mm x 420mm print is personally signed by the artist and is one of a limited edition of 850. A limited number are also available signed by John Surtees himself. He remains the only driver to have won World Championships on both two and four wheels.
https://www.dukevideo.com/prd8773/TT-Legends-John-Surtees-Print

John Surtees 1963 World Championship winning Ferrari 156

artwork by Alain Boudouin)

Insert a different letter of the alphabet into each of the 26 empty boxes to form words reading across. The letter you insert may be at the beginning, the end or the middle of the word. Each letter of the alphabet will be used only once. Cross off each letter in the list as you use it. All the letters in each row are not necessarily used in forming the word.

Example: In the first row, we have inserted the letter Z to form the word BENZOL

A B C D E F G H I J K L M N O P Q R S T U V W X Y Z̸

A	N	D	B	E	N	**Z**	O	L	E	I	J	W
Z	M	A	T	C	H		E	S	S	G	I	U
R	B	A	R	R	I		R	D	C	M	D	F
U	G	R	D	V	H		I	C	T	O	R	Y
B	X	W	G	E	N		R	Y	V	T	M	Z
N	N	O	R	T	O		F	L	D	N	V	K
T	H	U	N	D	E		P	V	R	W	B	V
C	G	H	R	E	D		A	N	B	H	G	D
H	Y	X	O	Y	R		R	O	K	E	N	O
N	X	F	E	J	Z		A	N	G	E	R	C
F	R	T	Z	Y	M		R	E	A	S	E	D
G	E	A	R	B	O		Z	B	L	T	D	J
X	M	T	L	A	P		I	N	G	H	Z	T
I	T	W	V	N	S		N	B	E	A	M	E
T	G	S	E	P	E		O	R	N	E	R	S
A	E	J	I	C	R		L	A	G	H	Z	F
Z	D	N	B	E	B		T	T	L	E	I	X
N	Q	Q	L	W	V		U	M	P	V	W	X
N	I	O	H	U	S		V	A	R	N	A	Q
S	N	A	R	R	O		Q	Z	O	S	V	Y
Q	K	E	J	X	T		R	E	S	D	S	Q
M	Z	A	Z	P	R		Z	E	C	G	Z	H
Q	H	J	H	M	A		O	R	P	J	M	U
C	E	X	W	W	O		D	S	G	E	P	G
B	G	T	Z	D	U		E	T	W	N	K	N
J	H	G	A	G	O		T	I	N	I	N	U

20

Giacomo Agostini is pictured in 1968 on his 500cc MV Agusta at the spot on the course that now bears his name - 'Ago's Leap'. Agostini's first victory came in the 1966 Junior and from 1968 to 1972 he won a further nine races. Prints are available:
https://www.dukevideo.com/prd8776/TT-Legends-Giacomo-Agostini-Print

Solve each clue to produce a word that will fit in the corresponding boxes.

ACROSS WORDS
1 - Famous Father And Son
2 - The Fight Becomes A ...
7 - It Waxes And Wanes
8 - Repeat
10 - Prima Donna
11 - Beatles Movie Of 1965
12 - A Short Jazz Passage
14 - Newly Received Information
15 - Dna Sequence In A Gene
16 - Sudden Pull
17 - Successful American Bike

22 - The Compound Is Very Import
23 - Successful Pre-war Bike
24 - One Of The Norton Riders
25 - It On Top Of The Trophy
26 - Japanese Giant

DOWN WORDS
1 - Stanley I Presume
3 - Be Lucky To Get These
4 - If Its Green Its A ...
5 - The Winner Takes This
6 - Its A Hairpin

9 - Hold On To These
13 - The Greatest Italian?
18 - Not Wide Here
19 - Bill Was Very Quick
20 - Silver And Black Tank
21 - The Turn Into A Corner

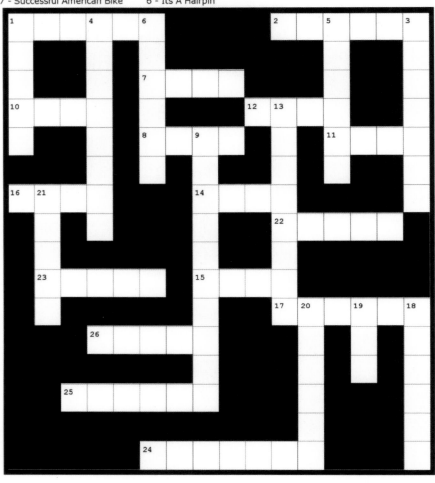

Mike Hailwood M.B.E. G.M., one of the all-time-greats of motorcycle sport history, depicted here at Quarterbridge in 1967 on the 500cc Honda-4. This race - the Senior TT - gave him his 12th TT win and completed his second hat-trick of victories. It was one of the greatest TT battles ever seen as Mike and Giacomo Agostini swapped the lead as they pushed their machines and themselves harder and harder. 'Mike the Bike' retired at the end of the year, but came back in 1978 and 1979 to bring his total wins to 14.

Each print has been signed by the artist and is one of a Limited Edition of 850. Size 594mm x 420mm. on fine art paper.

www.dukevideo.com/prd8775/Mike-Hailwood-TT-Legend-Print-Ltd-Ed-by-Peter-Hearsey

The spaces between the words in the following message have been eliminated and divided into pieces. Rearrange the pieces to reconstruct the messages. The dashes indicate the number of letters in each word.

```
EEN  TWA  IFI  EIS  DHA  STT  ERS
PTH  ERR  LAN  THA  DEV  EMO  CLA
STH
```

    — — — — — — —

    — — — — — — —

    — — — — — — — —

— — — — — — — — — — — —

    — — — — — — —

    — — — —

TT Sidecar greats **Dave Molyneux** and **Nick Crowe** battle in one of the most memorable, and closest, three-wheel races the Mountain course has ever seen, with Crowe and partner **Mark Cox** bringing the LCR Honda outfit home for victory just seconds ahead of the DMR Suzuki of Moly and **Daniel Sayle.** The three-lap grudge match in 2008 was the faring-bashing showdown between the two Manx TT greats that all fans had wanted to see. Sadly it would be the last time Crowe and Moly would go head-to-head over the Mountain course for a full race distance.

https://www.dukevideo.com/prd8847/Side-by-Side-TT-Sidecar-Dave-Molyneux-and-Nick-Crowe

The following words can be found in the diagram below reading forward, backward, up, down and diagonally. Find the words and circle them.

manager	finish
husqvarna	dixon
guthrie	walker
refueling	woods
tyres	miles
chain	suzuki

```
I R H U S Q V A R N A T I O V G
T O E U Z U T W O O D S W V I C
Y I U F S U Z U K I P B X Y Y D
R R Q G U U B O M D X G L M B S
E A M I L E S W R V P O R Y Q Z
S T F B Q D L A T V Q A Q R O C
U M J G Y L Y I Z H Q U X E L V
V L O A N E E N N Y A E Y Q V N
W T Q Z C W Y N V G X V M S S Q
A D H N M P B M C E G R P E R U
L D S I P Q B C H A I N G Q E D
K O I S Z M N L E F C R I T O X
E V N B Z B S P G K J J H S Z A
R D I X O N U G Q Y J F Q T I S
D U F W J W F C L C X M B Y U F
R E M A N A G E R P A O I A O G
```

This stunning print of Joey Dunlop, the most successful TT rider of all time, shows him negotiating Union Mills in 1985 on the 750cc Honda. Each 594mm x

420mm print is personally signed by the artist and is one of a limited edition of 850.

https://www.dukevideo.com/prd8777/TT-Legend-Joey-Dunlop-Print

A first-rate print based on a painting by Peter Hearsey. Joey Dunlop in A4 size - Yer Maun - is depicted in action wearing his famous yellow helmet and with the customary Number 3 on his Honda. The picture really conveys the feeling of speed and for Joey's legions of fans, this is a superb memento.

www.dukevideo.com/prd9912/Joey-Dunlop-Yer-Maun-A4-Print

Each of these Cryptograms is a message in substitution code. THE SILLY DOG might become UJD WQPPZ BVN if U is substituted for T, J for H, D for E, etc. One way to break the code is to look for repeated letters. E, T, A, O, N, R and I are the most often used letters. A single letter is usually A or I; OF, IS and IT are common 2-letter words; try THE or AND for a 3-letter group. The code is different for each Cryptogram.

1. Ci xrrvrn g qemruetr aetajbxcet isgi
   isrh yebjn yct isr mgar gugct

2. Shy zbko wqwdb swe ahki zgofyzzi
   cdj, nzf co sfzio eztb zb yco
   Jzhbywdb

3. Qss pgd jqbaeu mhwdmu fdmd ao pgd
   zmhw, qow qss pgd jqbaeu chtdu.

Steve Hislop is pictured at Sulby Bridge in 1992 on the rotary-engined 588cc Norton. On winning the 1992 Senior he set the fastest-ever race average speed at 121.38mph. It was just one of eleven TT victories for Hizzy, including hat-tricks in 1989 and 1991. Print: 594mm x 420mm

https://www.dukevideo.com/prd8780/Steve-Hislop-TT-Legend-Print

Insert a different letter of the alphabet into each of the 26 empty boxes to form words reading across. The letter you insert may be at the beginning, the end or the middle of the word. Each letter of the alphabet will be used only once. Cross off each letter in the list as you use it. All the letters in each row are not necessarily used in forming the word.

Example: In the first row, we have inserted the letter Z to form the word GUZZI

A B C D E F G H I J K L M N O P Q R S T U V W X Y ~~Z~~

M	Q	D	G	U	Z	**Z**	I	H	M	G	W	R
P	V	W	H	K	A		A	S	A	K	I	G
Z	L	Y	G	P	M		L	E	S	U	O	K
A	G	B	A	T	T		E	S	I	N	U	N
I	E	E	G	W	M		U	Z	U	K	I	Y
T	J	E	N	T	R		Z	A	G	L	Y	D
R	Y	M	Z	W	P		R	E	A	S	E	K
V	D	U	N	L	O		I	N	V	O	G	E
J	T	Z	H	R	A		S	E	Y	Z	O	C
T	K	S	N	A	E		E	L	L	Q	G	F
B	A	R	H	U	S		V	A	R	N	A	L
B	E	M	B	R	O		E	N	A	B	C	L
Y	D	C	R	A	S		H	H	G	B	E	W
X	A	S	P	E	C		A	T	O	R	S	R
I	N	V	A	S	C		S	T	R	O	L	G
G	J	S	Z	E	N		O	Y	U	J	G	A
D	V	H	E	R	M		S	I	V	L	U	I
I	S	B	O	S	R		A	D	C	T	F	C
U	R	G	U	T	H		I	E	T	U	F	V
C	U	X	W	O	O		S	P	X	G	C	G
P	E	P	L	T	W		I	C	T	O	R	Y
H	A	N	D	L	E		A	R	S	H	Y	C
L	B	O	W	A	C		I	D	E	N	T	J
Z	U	W	R	E	F		E	L	I	N	G	C
G	E	A	R	B	O		Q	Z	Z	K	E	V
O	Z	I	M	O	U		T	A	I	N	X	R

'King of the Mountain', John McGuinness. This exceptional artwork was unveiled during the 2009 TT, when the Morecambe missile notched up his 15th win – to become the second most successful rider ever around the Mountain circuit – and set a new outright lap record with a staggering average speed of 131.378mph for the 37¾-mile course.

This painting captures McGuinness on board the HM Plant Honda Superbike which carried him to his 13th TT victory during the Centenary TT Celebrations in 2007. This was also the machine on which McGuinness became the first man ever to lap the TT course at more than 130mph, with an average speed of 130.354mph. Prints are available here:
 https://www.dukevideo.com/prd8802/John-McGuinness-TT-Legend-Print

Fill all the empty squares with digits from 1 to 4 so that each digit appears once in each row and column. The digits in each outlined shape must also produce the number in the top left of the shape when they are all multiplied together. Digits may be repeated within area as long as just 1 of that number is in it's respective row and column.

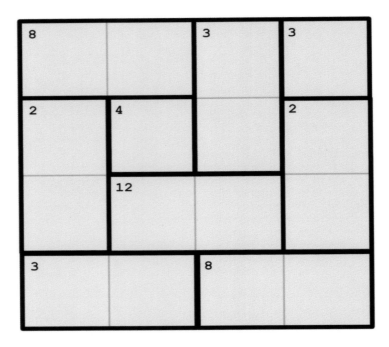

The day Michael Dunlop emulated his late father Robert and uncle Joey to claim victory at the Isle of Man TT. It shows him riding his 600cc Yamaha to victory in the second Supersport race at the 2009 TT.

Michael is shown sweeping through Creg-ny-Baa, with Kate's cottage in the background, echoing the many famous images of Robert and Joey Dunlop at the same point on the course during their illustrious road racing careers.

Celebrate the success of the new generation of the Dunlop name in road racing with this strictly limited edition print, signed by both Michael Dunlop and artist Peter Hearsey.

Print Size 594mm x 420mm.

https://www.dukevideo.com/prd8830X/Michael-s-First-Limited-Edition-Signed-Print

Solve each clue to produce a word that will fit in the corresponding boxes.

ACROSS WORDS
1 - Slippery Sam Was One
2 - The Winner Gets This
7 - Pale Or Greyish In Color
8 - Amphibian Without A Tail
9 - Instant Message
11 - Military Group
12 - Unit Of Paper
13 - _____ Of The Week
15 - Get The Creases Out Of
16 - Of Water, Blue/green
17 - Border

18 - These Are Not Red
19 - Small But Very Fast
23 - Require
24 - Pre-war Super Star
25 - The 50's Star Rider
26 - Japanese Rice Wine
27 - The Yellow Cab Is This

DOWN WORDS
1 - Unwelcome Loud Noise
3 - Japanese Bikes
4 - To Others

5 - Pole With A Flat Blade
6 - You Always Need This
10 - Never On Purpose
14 - Handsome And Very Quick
20 - The Star British Bike ?
21 - Sign Of Tiredness
22 - Go Nowhere Without This.
28 - Motes

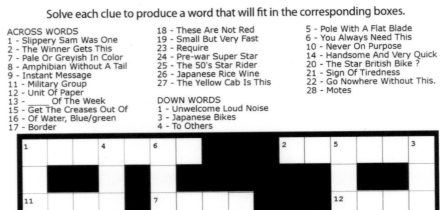

The supreme skill of the late David Jefferies was captured on canvas by renowned motorsport artist Peter Hearsey and was due to be launched at TT2003 by DJ. Sadly, this was not to be, but the Jefferies family nevertheless encouraged us to publish this fine tribute to DJ's mastery of the TT course with their support. The 594mm x 420mm print captures David Jefferies blasting through Rhencullen on his way to victory in the 2002 Duke Formula One TT aboard his TAS Suzuki. During the race he obliterated his previous 125mph lap record with an incredible 126.68mph lap.

Limited edition - 850 numbered prints. Printed on fine art paper and signed by the artist.

https://www.dukevideo.com/prd8785/David-Jefferies-TT-Legend-Print-Limited-Edition-by-Peter-Hearsey

The following words can be found in the diagram below reading forward, backward, up, down and diagonally. Find the words and circle them.

signpost   walker
cylinder   chain
simpson   danger
start   engine
practice   grease
trophy   fuel

```
A  N  P  Z  Z  Q  W  T  W  Q  A  K  K  L  Q  P
T  M  J  J  B  M  S  F  Y  V  A  W  A  W  R  A
S  J  F  E  A  X  U  A  W  K  W  Q  G  A  N  N
O  G  U  Q  R  Y  C  H  L  L  Q  S  C  M  X  O
P  R  E  J  S  W  F  S  S  F  P  T  T  P  T  S
N  E  L  U  N  U  J  Y  R  I  A  A  E  E  P
G  A  Q  V  D  S  D  O  D  C  T  R  B  B  D  M
I  S  T  Y  I  L  R  R  E  O  A  T  K  D  U  I
S  E  E  Q  H  Z  E  A  F  Q  A  K  V  R  G  S
Y  K  J  M  O  D  D  O  P  H  H  O  P  W  T  F
E  T  P  H  N  O  U  Y  W  T  Y  B  J  A  Y  M
E  Q  S  I  I  D  A  B  Q  O  F  E  D  L  M  L
S  C  L  E  A  X  G  Y  N  N  N  H  M  K  J  A
K  Y  K  J  H  J  X  O  Z  P  R  Z  R  E  I  N
C  X  M  R  C  J  Y  J  M  Y  H  P  O  R  T  D
G  S  D  A  N  G  E  R  E  N  G  I  N  E  B  U
```

Each of these Cryptograms is a message in substitution code. THE SILLY DOG might become UJD WQPPZ BVN if U is substituted for T, J for H, D for E, etc. One way to break the code is to look for repeated letters. E, T, A, O, N, R and I are the most often used letters. A single letter is usually A or I; OF, IS and IT are common 2-letter words; try THE or AND for a 3-letter group. The code is different for each Cryptogram.

1. Sglp gev odablv bldp reis tu odenstnl, fws gev gev e retd ejawus ar jlngeutneh sdawfhl.

2. Yu lasck zv o zouucv zvulvvm ufv pash-euhaive omk ula-euhaive

3. Eb tiv icvurgqbrj pgrr cuzb, priq ud qeb qids ido gvbo bhbzj ldme up qeb zuio

Insert a different letter of the alphabet into each of the 26 empty boxes to form words reading across. The letter you insert may be at the beginning, the end or the middle of the word. Each letter of the alphabet will be used only once. Cross off each letter in the list as you use it. All the letters in each row are not necessarily used in forming the word.

Example: In the first row, we have inserted the letter Z to form the word SUZUKI

A B C D E F G H I J K L M N O P Q R S T U V W X Y Z̸

H	M	E	S	S	U	**Z**	U	K	I	N	O	N
P	C	M	T	D	R		U	E	L	R	U	J
M	O	B	P	R	A		T	I	C	E	C	Z
Y	I	T	H	U	N		E	R	J	T	B	Z
J	U	R	N	Q	T		I	C	T	O	R	Y
Y	R	S	R	F	G		E	N	Z	O	L	I
O	Z	C	A	G	U		T	A	B	C	G	D
F	T	P	E	S	C		A	I	N	Y	N	L
J	A	Q	B	U	N		A	L	O	W	R	N
N	X	O	L	Y	A		A	H	A	K	A	L
G	U	L	R	E	F		E	L	I	N	G	A
S	X	S	M	K	A		A	S	A	K	I	E
R	D	V	H	U	S		V	A	R	N	A	B
B	K	S	P	A	R		P	L	U	G	X	K
S	L	Q	F	G	U		H	R	I	E	B	O
H	E	N	W	D	I		O	N	E	Q	X	H
T	M	D	D	W	O		D	S	C	Q	F	N
X	P	A	G	R	A		T	P	Y	C	Z	H
W	T	R	O	P	H		B	A	H	S	F	J
C	E	N	G	I	N		P	F	V	N	R	Z
E	H	Z	T	H	C		A	S	H	O	S	J
B	K	N	M	A	N		G	E	R	D	A	E
K	I	R	B	A	N		O	M	V	K	P	N
N	Q	Y	A	S	W		I	T	S	T	P	J
K	N	C	X	T	W		A	P	P	I	N	G
Z	M	O	I	N	D		A	N	O	S	J	B

Answer Key

From Page 6

```
S X E L H V C B J Z O P J M X A
R I Z T S M M J R Z O F M N C K
O V A B P W Y T H G T P J C H D
T Y Z J V P T I M S Y B I F F O
A N O W N D C Z R N R D A S C O
T W R R V E X L O E I K Y A A W
C R E I N K K S G N S P Y H L L
E L D L O L C N T B L V D I N I
P Z M M K L I B P W Z P W R Y A
S J A B N R J B R H J D T U R H
E X N T I P T W X G W K R E H M
G D L F A W Z D U I F E K N X L
U A S E H O S J M L Z G I T X N
E I H E C M T L P N E K O R B F
M H P J C Y O G I L R C M Y W R
E S P E E D G E Q T R O P H Y F
```

From Page 8

1. Vnaczakch bnn owpb K vawpuzs kcbn buz lwcg, xwp xkcszs wcs bnaz ym qzwbuzap lwsqm

   Cornering too fast I crashed into the bank, was winded and tore my leathers badly

2. Mwzu wej qkxbzj bzku lerm da qkegmdgz, fnm wej wej e ledk esxnam xl szgweadgeo mkxnfoz.

   They had proved very fast in practice, but had had a fair amount of mechanical trouble.

3. Mxx uew amqktz bjswbz pwbw kv uew ibjs, mvs mxx uew amqktz gjfwz.

   All the famous riders were on the grid, and all the famous bikes.

```
U W H B E N Z O L H R I L
T Q S D X Y E N T R Y V W
V C P R E D M A N W D T O
P B I D R O B E N N E T T
F M H A I R P I N J Q S E
B P Z R O A D O G H M X W
E L B P O S I T I O N A E
X W M A T C H L E S S Y D
F Y I R R E C O R D T G K
R T H O S E J E C T C L N
V H I R T H U N D E R N U
W E A T H E R S N W V C T
K U J H U S Q V A R N A B
V K Y E N P F U E L S T O
W A C P F I N I S H D N C
O N A R R O W P A C M V E
N L F V O I L T C F R Y D
L A P P I N G A L I H W K
Q H A I L W O O D X U R V
G E A R B O X F T B M O X
G S W J G R A I N F S Z W
N J S U Z U K I R B Y K U
X T R O P H Y Z X V M O Q
K A M O U N T A I N Y N Q
A E N E O H V I C T O R Y
S U R T E E S Y W H U W K
```

From Page 10

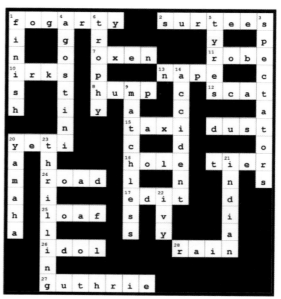

From Page 12

39

From Page 14

s o   t h e   n o r t o n

w i n n i n g

s e q u e n c e

w a s   d i s t u r b e d

b y   a n   e x - m e m b e r

o f   t h e i r

o w n   t e a m .

From Page 16

```
L Q Y D L L E F E A N S J D G A
O A Z W S Y N J V L A Z X S A G
Q C P D K Q U Z E T G H W K G R
A U K P G U Z F Q S U Z U K I A
S D P R I Z E E B Z S P A W I N
B N K E Y N B Z X F T T F C D T
M C Y X J T G W P K A P T O Q S
D R P M S C S W X B X W Z D Q F
F T R H S P R S L L G V B Z J R
R N I G Z B J W E Z K U V K X L
P D F H K Y W C J L I O I I E P
J H O A Z B J F A L H O X K Z E
R G J P R Y S X G D V C C F E T
K O J T T R A C K V X U T U Z R
E A A H O N D A P P X Z P A P O
F Y E E M M A R G O R D X X M L
```

From Page 18

1. Utt xjv kuylzh bgwvbh qvbv ls xjv
cbgw, usw uff xjv kuylzh ogpvh.

> All the famous riders were on the grid, and all
> the famous bikes.

2. Xsrur fur tra viflrw asrur xsr upcr
pw qjx dfqgrc jyru jqr wpcr ju xsr
jxsru.

> There are few places where the rider is not
> banked over one side or the other.

3. G eseryugd fdgjos agn fdghsw rb kps
agdd rffrnuks kps nkgyk dubs.

> A memorial plaque was placed on the wall
> opposite the start line.

From Page 20

```
A N D B E N Z O L E I J W
Z M A T C H L E S S G I U
R B A R R I E R D C M D F
U G R D V H V I C T O R Y
B X W G E N T R Y V T M Z
N N O R T O N F L D N V K
T H U N D E R P V R W B V
C G H R E D M A N B H G D
H Y X O Y R B R O K E N O
N X F E J Z D A N G E R C
F R T Z Y M G R E A S E D
G E A R B O X Z B L T D J
X M T L A P P I N G H Z T
I T W V N S U N B E A M E
T G S E P E C O R N E R S
A E J I C R F L A G H Z F
Z D N B E B A T T L E I X
N Q Q L W V H U M P V W X
N I O H U S Q V A R N A Q
S N A R R O W Q Z O S V Y
Q K E J X T Y R E S D S Q
M Z A Z P R I Z E C G Z H
Q H J H M A J O R P J M U
C E X W W O O D S G E P G
B G T Z D U K E T W N K N
J H G A G O S T I N I N U
```

From Page 22

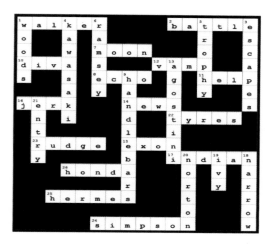

From Page 24

that was

the most

terrific

lap the island

had ever

seen

From Page 30

Page 32

8		3	3
4	**2**	**1**	**3**
2	4		2
2	**4**	**3**	**1**
	12		
1	**3**	**4**	**2**
3		8	
3	**1**	**2**	**4**

From Page 34

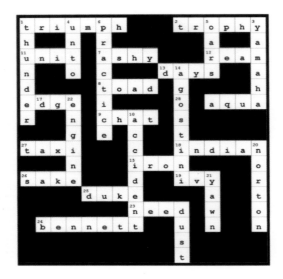

From Page 36

From Page 37

1. Sglp gev odablv bldp reis tu
odenstnl, fws gev gev e retd ejawu
ar jlngeutneh sdawfhl.

   They had proved very fast in practice, but had
   had a fair amount of mechanical trouble.

2. Yu lasck zv o zouucv zvulvvm ufv
pash-euhaive omk ula-euhaive

   It would be a battle between the four-strokes
   and two-strokes

3. Eb tiv icvurgqbrj pgrr cuzb, priq
qeb qids ido gvbo bhbzj ldme up qe
zuio

   He was absolutely full bore, flat on the tank
   and used every inch of the road

From Page 38

H	M	E	S	S	U	**Z**	U	K	I	N	O	N
P	C	M	T	D	R	F	U	E	L	R	U	J
M	O	B	P	R	A	C	T	I	C	E	C	Z
Y	I	T	H	U	N	D	E	R	J	T	B	Z
J	U	R	N	Q	T	V	I	C	T	O	R	Y
Y	R	S	R	F	G	B	E	N	Z	O	L	I
O	Z	C	A	G	U	S	T	A	B	C	G	D
F	T	P	E	S	C	H	A	I	N	Y	N	L
J	A	Q	B	U	N	G	A	L	O	W	R	N
N	X	O	L	Y	A	M	A	H	A	K	A	L
G	U	L	R	E	F	U	E	L	I	N	G	A
S	X	S	M	K	A	W	A	S	A	K	I	E
R	D	V	H	U	S	Q	V	A	R	N	A	B
B	K	S	P	A	R	K	P	L	U	G	X	K
S	L	Q	F	G	U	T	H	R	I	E	B	O
H	E	N	W	D	I	X	O	N	E	Q	X	H
T	M	D	D	W	O	O	D	S	C	Q	F	N
X	P	A	G	R	A	N	T	P	Y	C	Z	H
W	T	R	O	P	H	Y	B	A	H	S	F	J
C	E	N	G	I	N	E	P	F	V	N	R	Z
E	H	Z	T	H	C	R	A	S	H	O	S	J
B	K	N	M	A	N	A	G	E	R	D	A	E
K	I	R	B	A	N	J	O	M	V	K	P	N
N	Q	Y	A	S	W	P	I	T	S	T	P	J
K	N	C	X	T	W	L	A	P	P	I	N	G
Z	M	O	I	N	D	I	A	N	O	S	J	B

Recommended TT Reading:

Racing Round the Island - Bob Holliday.

100 Years of The Isle of Man TT – David Wright.

TT Mixture – David Wright.

The Story of the TT – G.S. Davison.

That Near-Death Thing – Rick Broadbent.

Built for Speed – John McGuinness.

Roar Racer – Michael Dunlop.

TT Titans – Matthew Richardson.

The Motocourse History of the TT – Nick Harris

Joey Dunlop – His Authorised Biography.

Mike the Bike Again – Ted Macauley.

Geoff Duke. The Stylish Champion – Mick Walker.

John Surtees. My Incredible life on Two and Four Wheels.

Freddie Dixon. The man with a heart of a lion – David Mason.

Giacomo Agostini. Champion of Champions – Mick Walker.

The Little Book of the T.T – Duke Marketing

If you are interested in learning more about my other products and publications, please visit www.racingbooks.org
Please feel free to join my mailing list. On Facebook at AutosUK and Twitter AutosUK_

Available on Amazon and at
https://www.ebay.co.uk/str/theautomobiliacentre

All the artwork in this book can be viewed and purchased from: https://www.dukevideo.com/Isle-of-Man-TT

Best wishes and thanks for your interest

Steve Bradley

Aka Max.M. Power

Books 1 and 2 of A Fatal Addiction
The Seduction of Speed

" He was grinning as the car roared on to the Home Banking, flashed under the Members' Bridge and across the white timing line. His last thoughts were that the lap must have been much better than 120mph.

Then, as he came into full view of the packed paddock, the engine unable to take any more abuse gave up the struggle and blew apart."

https://www.amazon.co.uk/dp/1916491022

The Triumphs and the Tragedies

"The unpleasant smell that invaded him when he finally managed to open the door was a mixture of dampness and decay. His torch illuminated a layer of inky black water, much as he had been expecting, but as he moved the light across the slick surface, he noticed a flash of white. He concentrated the beam on the spot and an involuntary shriek of terror left his mouth. The sockets of an eyeless skull were looking up, straight at him"

https://www.amazon.co.uk/dp/1916491049

About the Author

Maxwell Mark Power was born to the sound of screaming racing engines.
His family lived just one mile from the Hanger Straight (as the crow flies) at Silverstone and it was British Grand Prix day.

Max grew up in a comfortable home with every spare space containing huge stacks of old Motor Sport and Autosport magazines and Motoring and Motorcycle Newspapers. Little wonder in his early years he thought motoring was the real world...the rest just strange.
His mother said his first word had been Mummy; in fact, it had been. money.
Even at this young age, Max knew that if he wanted to be a racing driver, he would need lots of. money.
With single-minded determination, persistence and some skill Max did become a successful racing motorist firstly on motorbikes then with racing cars.

Max did enjoy win many races, but constant shortage of money and some HUGE crashes insured he never made the "big time". A few times he has tried to retire from racing, but his addiction would always drag him back to the sport he loves.
He now lives alone in his large workshop in the East of England surrounded by his trophies from old glories and bits of broken racing cars.
However, he is still an optimist.

His motto " Where's the next race, I'm going to win this time"

Printed in Poland
by Amazon Fulfillment
Poland Sp. z o.o., Wrocław